The Preposterous God

Book #2 in the Little Book Series

Kent Philpott
Katie Philpott

EVP

The Preposterous God

ISBN: 978-1-946794-08-6

Library of Congress Control Number: 2018960066

Cover and interior design by KLC Philpott

All Biblical Scripture quotations, unless otherwise indicated, are taken from the Holy Bible, English Standard Version® (ESV®), copyright © 2001 by Crossway Bibles, a publishing ministry of Good News Publishers. All rights reserved.

Contents

Preface

We don't get very far when we attempt to figure out what or who God is.

I have no idea, or almost no idea, of what or who God is. And I am a Christian who believes the Bible; I have several degrees plus ten years of theological seminary culminating in a doctorate. I have also been a pastor for more than forty-five years and consider myself a preacher of the Gospel.

When I read my Bible, I discover what God did. The short version of that story is summed up in The Apostles' Creed. He (and He is a She as well, which can be argued based upon Genesis 1:27[1]) is unlike any he or she we have ever known.[2]

He created everything that exists, was actually present in the Garden of Eden on day one, communicated with the man and the woman, and then, due to a major problem, sent them away. Theologically, we know why the Creator took this drastic course of action. Sin, which is

---

[1] In this book I capitalize pronouns referring to the Trinity, thus He and Him. The English Standard Version of the Bible used throughout does not so capitalize.

[2] We do not need to get excited about the fact that the ancients did not have the sensibilities about gender issues that we do today. The authors of Scripture were people of their day, not ours.

the breaking of the God's Law, cannot be united with Him. There has never been, nor will there ever be, sin in the direct presence of God.

This is therefore the reason why the rebel, Satan, was cast out of heaven. This is the reason Adam and Eve were sent out of the garden as well. Heaven, an utterly unimaginable realm, is where God dwells in utter holiness, meaning that no unholiness can be in His presence. This is an image or concept we will never understand, at least while on the planet.

A confession is due right now. Early in my Christian walk I did not question what the Bible says about God. Now, with fifty-five years at the time of this writing of walking with Jesus, I question my preposterous God more than ever before. I am confident I can do so knowing I am not in danger of losing my salvation. Then again, I am past the stage when I worry about what others might think when I raise serious issues about fundamental elements of the Faith. But most of all I think this book comes out of knowing God more completely than ever before. My child-like faith has grown up enough to the point I grasp the enormity, at least from a human stand point, of the absurdity of the God of the Bible. For me, this Little Book had to be written for myself and others like me who dare to bring up the big issues.

God is preposterous. The *Oxford Concise Dictionary* uses the words "absurd, outrageous, contrary to nature, reason, or common sense" to define the term.

These attempts do not go far enough when it comes to what and who God is. After all, they are merely terms we understand, and if we are honest, we will admit that our understandings are very limited. We are not on equal terms with God, we will not become God, we will not be absorbed into God, nor will we have union with God.

God is preposterous, even while we wish He were not. We keep trying to whittle Him down, reduce Him, or find a formula for Him, but it will not work.

May we allow ourselves to ask the question, "What and who is God?"

Chapter One

The Creator

That some entity created all there is, meaning the entire universe, is unimaginable.

It has been postulated that the universe just is, that it exists with no Creator necessary, that the universe is simply the fundamental reality, without need for a Creator, a first cause. No god or goddess, no Mind, no Consciousness, no Singularity, no Strings attached—it is what it is.

Of course, this leaves a lot to be explained, if indeed, there is something that needs explaining. Maybe acceptance of such an ultimate reality is as close to actualization as a human being can get. But is this a mindset placed by God?

The history of humankind, what little we know of it, illustrates that most of us on the planet have a sense of a Being, often called God, or called something else but with the same essence. Does this prove there is a God? Certainly not! We can all be completely wrong.

A Major Confrontation

Some time in the past a series of legends or genera-tional stories began circulating among an ancient people known as the *A'bru*.[1] Eventually, they were committed to writing during the time of Moses, in the mid-second millennium before the common era, a date of approximately 1500 BCE.

The earliest accounts of these are recorded in the book called the Hebrew Bible. There are multiple versions of what we refer to as "creation accounts" in the first book of this Bible.[2] One begins in Genesis 1:1 and runs through Genesis 2:3.[3] Here the word for the Creator is transliterated as Elohim or El.[4]

The second account begins at Genesis 2:4 and runs through Genesis 3:24 or 4:26, depending on one's view. The third is merely the first two verses of chapter [5]:

> This is the book of the generations of Adam. When God created man, he made him in the likeness of God. Male and female he created

---

[1]   *A'bru* is only an approximate spelling. In time the word Hebrew was used to denote this primitive Middle Eastern tribe whose origins are unknown.

[2]   Some insist there is only one creation account, others say three. I am among the latter.

[3]   The chapter and verse designations were added during the common era, about mid 2nd millennium. Some errors were made in assigning verse numbers, as is obvious to those who study the Scripture.

[4]   To transliterate is to use, as here, English letter equivalents for Hebrew letters.

them, and he blessed them and named them
Man when they were created. (Genesis 5:1–2)

The first account reads: "In the beginning, God created
the heavens and the earth" (Genesis 1:1). "Beginning"
is assumed to mean the creation of the universe, since
the passage goes on to describe, blow by blow, how
all there is came to be. An ancient and poetic description of the process may be seen in the account, yet the
basics are plain. Verse 27 says: "So God created man
in his own mage, in the image of God he created him;
male and female he created them." This verse is very
similar to that of Genesis 5:1–2 quoted above.

The second account translates the Hebrew Yahweh as
God, thus distinguishing this account from the first. The
first is thought to be the oldest of the three, because
the word Yahweh came into use during the time of
Moses, as is evident from Exodus chapter 3. The first
verse of the second creation account is: "These are the
generations of the heavens and the earth when they
were created, in the day that the LORD5 God made the
earth and the heavens" (Genesis 2:4).

The Creator

It all starts with the Creator. Either there is a Creator, or
all of existence is a mystery.

---

5   The large and small caps combination of "LORD"
indicates the underlying Hebrew word is *Yahweh*.

How does one know what is what? Ecclesiastes 3:11 gives a credible answer:

> He has put eternity into man's heart, yet so that he cannot find out what God has done from the beginning to the end.

Solomon, the likely author of the verse, stated poetically the human condition that resonates with us, because we have an awareness of the truth expressed. However, all we need to do is look around us at the world in which we live to see something supremely gigantic and quite preposterous yet real, which tells us there is more than the eye can see.

Theologians call this "general revelation," and it is shared by all human beings. This may explain why history confirms that human beings have always had a "god sense" about them that turns into religion. Yet, there is a built-in limit.

In the eighth century before the common era, the prophet Isaiah clouded the waters. Yahweh, the personal name of the God of Israel—the El or Elohim—revealed to Isaiah the following:

> For my thoughts are not your thoughts, neither are your ways my ways, declares the LORD. For as the heavens are higher than the earth, so are my ways higher than your ways and my thoughts than your thoughts.

Mystery indeed! Eternity is placed into humans, but there is a limitation placed there by the Creator.

Adam and Eve

Whether one believes in a literal Adam and Eve is irrelevant, at least to many of us Bible believers. I myself do believe in an actual Adam and Eve who were the first truly human creatures and that they did not evolve from lower or more ancient organic forms. In addition, I suspect their creation to be rather recent, as geological time goes. My sense is that the evolutionary process implanted into all living forms simply could not develop a creature made in God's image. And we will continue the concept of "image" in the next chapter.

Chapter Two

The Created in the Image of the Creator

It is no wonder we are tempted to think of ourselves more highly than we ought. We are created in the very image of God. Image. What is this? When we look in a mirror, we certainly don't see God, who does not look like we do; this is easily concluded.

What, then, does "created in the image of God" mean? We see from the biblical account that it took both the male and the female to express something of the nature of God: "So God created man in his own image, in the image of God he created him; male and female he created them" (Genesis 1:27).

But "image" has much more to it than mere physical attributes.

We note that none of the animals God created, as depicted in Genesis chapter two, had a personal relationship with their Creator. That ability or status was reserved for the humans, Adam and Eve. Their relationship with God was personal to the extent that God actually communicated directly with this first couple. We see this in Genesis 3:8–13 after they disobeyed His one commandment:

And they heard the sound of the LORD God walking in the garden in the cool of the day, and the man and his wife hid themselves from the presence of the LORD God among the trees of the garden. But the LORD God called to the man and said to him, "Where are you?" And he said, "I heard the sound of you in the garden, and I was afraid, because I was naked, and I hid myself." He said, "Who told you that you were naked? Have you eaten of the tree of which I commanded you not to eat?" The man said, "The woman whom you gave to be with me, she gave me fruit of the tree, and I ate." Then the LORD God said to the woman, "What is this that you have done?" The woman said, "The serpent deceived me, and I ate."

Image therefore takes on the idea of the capacity to have fellowship with, to know and be known by, and to communicate with, the Creator. This idea may seem strange, even preposterous to us, yet it is at the heart of the ultimate intention of the Creator. There is a lot more to the story. Genesis, after all, means beginning.

God Incarnate

Is the garden appearance a case of God becoming incarnate—physically present? Christian thinkers have been divided on this issue for the last two thousand years. The passage quoted in Genesis 3 above

13

seems to indicate that an actual, physical Being was present in the Garden (Paradise) and literally spoke with Adam and Eve.

While the writer of the passage might have taken literary license and conveyed a most complex event into a manner more easily understood, there are also other possibilities, yet the minimum clear statement is that we find the Creator in real and actual conversation with a man and a woman. The Creator never spoke to any of the animals we find listed in Genesis chapter two, verses 18 through 23. But with Adam and Eve He did.

A Lonely Creator?

It has been suggested that the Creator was lonely, which prompted Him to create humans in order to have someone with whom to communicate and have a relationship. Neither the living organisms nor the angels satisfied Him, so fellowship would depend upon a Creature somewhat like Himself, a creature made in His image. Perhaps fellowship with human beings was the ultimate intention of the Creator. Perhaps He put that same desire for fellowship with Him inside of each human being.

Image—we humans are made in the image of the Creator. Do you ever have a sense of this? Have you read the writings of poets, heard the music of great composers, seen the paintings and sculpture of artists, or watched the films of talented directors, and seen the deep longings that abide in the spirit of men and women? Have you found in those creations the sound of a cry to know the Creator of all? The Creator is not lonely, as He is complete in His Being. However, we humans have a deep inner loneliness that can only be assuaged by a relationship with Him.

A Different Reason

We may never know why we are created in His image, and we may not really need to know. But just maybe the answer is that He loves us.

I can hear it now—the retort that the Creator can't possibly love His creation. After all, look at the world and see the suffering throughout history. We are born and we die, and in between is turmoil and strife, with our best hope being a painless death. If love is the reason, then why the evil loosed upon us?

The Creator's love is preposterous to us, given what we see in the world.

Chapter Three

The Creator and Evil

"Now the serpent was more crafty than any other beast of the field that the LORD God had made" (Genesis 3:1).

The serpent, as we find elsewhere in the Bible, is Satan, an angel who rebelled against the Creator.[1] We also know him as the devil, the commander of demons. Paul wrote to the church at Corinth: "But I am afraid that as the serpent deceived Eve by his cunning, your thoughts will be led astray from a sincere and pure devotion to Christ" (2 Corinthians 11:3).

Satan is a creature, as were all the other angels. C.S. Lewis recognized this and wrote, "There is no uncreated being except God."[2] And who created Satan? None other than the Creator God. How preposterous!

Satan has another name as well—Lucifer—which may be translated, "Day Star." This information is from Isaiah, the prophet who wrote in the eighth century before the common era. Here is what he said:

How you are fallen from heaven, O Day Star,

---

[1]   See Ezekiel 28:11–19; Revelation 12:7–10; and 20:1–3.

[2]   *The Screwtape Letters*, p. vii.

son of Dawn! How you are cut down to the ground, you who laid the nations low! You said in your heart, "I will ascend to heaven, above the stars of God I will set my throne on high, I will sit on the mount of assembly in the far reaches of the north; I will ascend above the heights of the clouds, I will make myself like the Most High. But you are brought down to Sheol, to the far reaches of the pit." (Isaiah 14:12–15)

The striving for power, authority, and adulation on the part of a created being/angel is at the heart of human history; it moved from Adam and Eve to Cain and on down to us. This is a thoroughly biblical worldview.

Theodicy—The Problem of Evil

David Hume, the eighteenth-century Scottish philosopher, captured the core of the puzzle in *Dialogues Concerning Natural Religion*. Attempting to define our impulse to question God on the matter of the presence of evil, Hume wrote: "He is willing to prevent evil, but not able? Then is he impotent. Is he able, but not willing? Then is he malevolent. Is he both able and willing: whence then is evil?"

Questions

The questions could go on and on with no satisfying

answer. The real question, however, is whether our questions require an answer. The Scripture, both the Hebrew and Greek portions, from Genesis to Revelation, make no attempt to confront the problem of evil; it merely assumes and acknowledges it with no explanations given. Evil is assumed, with its root cause being a creature who rebelled against the Creator at some unknown point, inside or outside of time. This knowledge does not deter human inquiry, however; we are stuck on the notion of evil being a problem needing a solution.

Is it possible that we humans are not capable of true understanding here? Might the Creator not intend for us to understand? Would it change things, if He provided a solution? We would likely just continue on our way, making Satan either a friend or an enemy.

In a way, God has indeed given an answer to the problem of evil. As an answer to Hume, my view is that the Creator is both able and willing to subdue Lucifer. What's more, He has already dealt a victorious and deadly blow to Satan. This is what the work of Christ is all about!

The Beautiful Devil

Satan desires to be worshipped and has franchised his corporation out across the globe. Some submit to him directly and knowingly; others do so indirectly. We know of straight-on Satanic worship and also of the occult arts, bundled together under the broad spectrum of spiritism, magic, and divination. His presence and abilities are enough to turn a hyper-materialist into a super-naturalist in a flash. Once one experiences a demonic presence, one is never the same again.

Beautiful is the Day Star, so very attractive and powerful. He has miracles, signs and wonders, and real raw power. He delights to anoint his priests and priestesses with dark and sensational gifts. He counts his converts by the billions.

Satan would claim the authorship of evil, but though he is malevolence itself, he is ultimately impotent.

The Work of Messiah[3] Jesus

Before the foundation of our world and the entire universe, the Creator God both foreknew and predestined the course of the history of the entirety of the creation, both on the micro and macro level. If not, He is not God.

Slowly, and from our point of view, painfully slowly, He is allowing the entire script to be played out. This is revealed piece-meal in the Bible, with the first core prophetic revelation being stated directly in Genesis

---

[3]   Messiah, from the Hebrew, *meshiach*, means the Anointed One, leading to the Greek, *Christos*.

3:15. This statement is part of a longer narrative from verses 14–19 and is what the Creator said to the creature, the serpent:

> I will put enmity between you and the woman,
> and between your offspring and her offspring;
> he shall bruise your head, and you shall bruise
> his heel.

The "woman" is a type but always female. First came Eve, the prototype, then the nation Israel, then the remnant Israel, then finally the single woman, Mary, mother of Jesus called the Christ.

"Enmity" is stronger than the English word generally conveys and means warfare or deadly conflict. We see "he" refers to Satan, including his followers, those angels who sided with Lucifer in the cataclysmic rebellion.

"Your offspring," the Creator says, and these are the followers and worshippers of Satan, knowingly or unknowingly, both demon and human. Quite an army!

"Her offspring" is in the singular, "he shall bruise."

Her offspring deals a deadly head blow to "your offspring," which offspring is capable only of dealing a bruise on the heel.

The "he" is the Messiah, the Christ, the One appointed by the Creator to undo all that the serpent brought upon the creation. This is the fundamental theme of all the Bible. The apostle John summed it up by saying: "The reason the son of God appeared was to destroy the works of the devil" (1 John 3:18b).

The work of Satan is to induce humans to hide from their Creator because of their guilt and shame, which is the natural effect of sin. His plan is to blind and possess those who follow him, so they might be with him in eternal gloom and darkness. We all are rebels against God, whether we recognize it or not. Therefore, God acted to bring peace and freedom to His beloved creation.

This "plan of salvation" moved directly to the Roman cross on which Jesus was hung about AD 30 outside the walls of Jerusalem. As the old hymn so eloquently presents it, "Only His blood can wash away my sin" — the blood Jesus shed while on the cross.

Problem of Evil Solved?

The problem of evil is not solved, not satisfactorily answered, but understood to some degree. This must be enough for us this side of eternity.

Will the great question be answered when we are in the presence of God? I doubt it; any possible relevance will be negated. Joy will fill us to fullness.

Chapter Four

The Evictor

East of Eden is where the Creator sent Adam and Eve as a consequence of the breaking of one single commandment—not to eat the fruit of a tree found in the midst of the garden. Two specific trees were named: "the tree of the knowledge of good and evil" (see Genesis 2:9, 17) and "the tree of life" (see Genesis 2:9; 3:22, 24).

In Genesis chapter 3 is recorded what the Creator, about to become the Evictor, said to an unknown audience. In a manner akin to a stage play God said,

> Behold, the man has become like one of us in knowing good and evil. Now, lest he reach out his hand and take also of the tree of life and eat, and live forever—" therefore the LORD God sent him out from the garden of Eden to work the ground from which he was taken. He drove out the man, and at the east of the garden of Eden he placed the cherubim and a flaming sword that turned every way to guard the way to the tree of life. (Genesis 3:22–24)

In our previous chapter we dealt with the problem of evil, and here in Genesis we encounter evil again. There are perhaps hundreds of passages in the Bible that beg this central question. Now, however, the focus is on the incredible, preposterous event where God threw His precious creation, even that made in His own image, out into a wilderness.

Prophetic?

The Book of Genesis initiates the story of God and His creation. The grand themes are presented in this book of beginnings then run throughout the rest of the Bible like threads in a woven tapestry, all the way to the last book, Revelation.

Created in the Creator's image, evicted from a paradise, recreated and forgiven, then restored and returned to experience the heavenly Paradise—this is the story of Scripture.

Why the long journey? Must the creature go through the agony of the eviction from the garden? Did the Creator toss Adam and Eve out because of a single infraction?

The Trouble with Sin

In the Genesis account the problem was the breaking of a single commandment, the only one given. Adam and Eve did eat the forbidden fruit. They knew it, and God knew it. And then we find something utterly preposterous.

Something happened after they ate the fruit; Adam and Eve's eyes were opened as never before. Yes, they then had more knowledge, but only the knowledge that sin brings. The result was guilt and fear.

They hid from God. Suddenly they realized they were naked and sewed some fig leaves together. When God came calling in the cool of the day, they did not respond or greet Him. Why so?

The thing about God is that He is holy, meaning, without sin. Sin is the breaking of the divine commands. God is wholly other; He alone is sinless. We are not so, and we all know it. Even the psychopath, whose conscience is not working as it should, knows something is amiss. Adam and Eve knew they had sinned and created a lie to hide behind. "The woman whom you gave to be with me, she gave me fruit of the tree, and I ate." "The serpent deceived me, and I ate." Blame shifting and excuses!

Would this have happened if there had been no presence of evil? Again, God must have known what would happen; yet He allowed that evil to invade the very paradise He made for the first humans.

And we are living with it still. Indeed, nothing has changed from that day to this. We wrestle with guilt, fear, loneliness, and are angry about all that has been lost. Perhaps the phrase "separation anxiety" expresses our inner conflict.

The Creator made us, so He must have known the terrible emotional and spiritual distress that would come to all of us. Yet we are told He is a loving God.

Being God, could He not have simply pardoned the guilty pair? Could He not have thrown the serpent out, even destroy the fallen angel? If we think too much on these issues it will not bode well with us. We then plunge further into the pit of snakes and are bitten innumerable times.

I have a vague idea of what happened back at the beginning of the human race, and even have some understanding of why God had to take action. Too many of us over the centuries have come up with simplistic answers to the age-old mystery, none of which gave much comfort. Often the easy answers create more questions than they solve.

No Easy Answer

First, do we have it right? Can we trust the Genesis account? We must ask these questions, even if fear would prevent it, and there are reasons to fear. Others might think we are off track, disobedient, cultic, rebellious, liberal, making shipwreck of our faith, or have gone apostate. These immaturities must be rejected, and we must explore reality regardless of pressures not to.

If I only had the Genesis material, I would wonder. But

all through Scripture, no character or author disputes it. The historians, the poets, the prophets, the apostles, Jesus' enemies, and Jesus Himself all adhere to the biblical account we have in Genesis. The systematic theology springing out of the Scripture demands that the early account of creation and eviction forms the necessary glue that holds together everything following it.

If Genesis is not accurate, Jesus died for nothing. He died for a preposterous something, all right. He died because our personal sin has separated us from the Creator, and only by our Lord Jesus taking our sin upon Himself can we once again walk in Paradise with our Creator. It is that simple.

Chapter Five

The Law Maker and Judge

Since God is the Law Maker, He has the right to be the Judge as well. The preposterous God of the Bible started out by giving one commandment, and when that commandment was broken, judgment followed swiftly. We have been suffering ever since.

Is it wrong of us to want to judge God, even be angry with Him for what has happened to us as a result? Is the God who judged our ancestors so harshly for breaking one little law a loving God? Is this the profile of a God who demands worship?

On this side of eternity no one will answer the questions above to any degree of satisfaction. I certainly cannot, and I have puzzled over these issues for decades. I have finally given up trying to judge God and am moving steadily toward realizing, more than ever before, that the God of Scripture is nothing less than absurd—meaning, I now know I have no hope of understanding Him as He truly is.

More and more laws

One commandment, then ten He gave Moses on Mount

Sinai. Briefly they are: no worshipping other gods, no making of images of other gods, no taking God's name in vain, must remember to rest on the Sabbath day, must honor father and mother, no murdering, committing adultery, stealing, bearing false witness, or coveting things belonging to a neighbor (Exodus 20:1–17).

There were plenty more given as time went on, which can be found in the rest of Exodus, then in Leviticus, Numbers, and Deuteronomy. Enough to make your head swim. Who could keep them? No one—which makes it clear that from then until now we all are law breakers and essentially condemned as a result.

After some period, around 1500 BCE, two general statements developed that summarized or encapsulated the myriad of laws. In Deuteronomy 6:5 we find, "You shall

Love the LORD your God with all your heart and with all your soul and with all you might." Then Leviticus 19:18 says, "You shall love your neighbor as yourself: I am the LORD."

That sounds nice, but it actually moved from really difficult to impossible, and no matter how one defines "love," the skimpiest expression of less than that would make anyone a law breaker, because we are surely not able to do what the Law Maker and Judge mandated.

Maybe I can keep, or at least try hard to keep, some of the ten commandments of Exodus 20. But the two love commandments? Can I do this? No.

How does God know when His commands are broken?

We have numerous sheriffs and cops, and they often catch someone breaking a law. Sometimes they do not. They cannot be everywhere watching and observing everything done under the sun. But the Bible's God has managed to peer into the hearts and minds of us all, all of the time. How could this be? It is unimaginable that even a Creator God could do this. He would have to be everywhere all the time and recording it all somehow. Do you see why the title of this Little Book is *The Preposterous God*?

We have no chance

"Let him who is without sin among you be the first to throw a stone at her" (John 8:7).

These are the words of Jesus spoken to religious leaders who had caught a woman in the act of committing adultery. She deserved death according to their law. By bringing the woman to Jesus, these righteous men sought to put Jesus on the spot. (Notice the other person, the man, did not appear.) After hearing Jesus say what He did, they walked away. At least, despite the evil intent of their hearts, they knew they were not without sin.

Only the liar or the deranged claims to be without sin. I often say that an hour does not go by that I have not in some way or another broken a law of God. I am not all that loving, I must admit. I am eager to judge and demean others, even if it is nothing more than a thought that flits through the grey matter. I find that I am biased, quick to assume the worst about someone, and in my conversation hold people up to a false light. Then there are perverse thoughts that flow through my mind on an almost daily basis.

Sure, I am a decent person, and I hope to do good things. Likely, I am as good as the next person, sometimes even better, but to what effect?

Look at what we find in His book: "For all have sinned and fall short of the glory of God" (Romans 3:23). That's it, and no amount of good deeds will change that. One sin is enough—just like what happened to Adam and Eve in the garden. One little bite, and it was "east of Eden" for them.

Two chapters later in Romans it gets worse: "For the wages of sin is death" (Romans 6:23a). Being sent away from the Creator was a kind of death, the death of being excluded from the presence of God, forever. Not a cessation of life, which would be easy, even acceptable. No, it's a continuation of being but with an everlasting sentence devoid of any good Presence.

From death to life

There is however Romans 6:23b: "But the gift of God is eternal life in Christ Jesus our Lord." No wonder we

Christians use the term "Gospel" when referring to the core message of our faith. The word simply means "Good News." Since the bad news is that we have broken the Creator's laws and would deserve death, instead He gives us the gift—and notice it is the word "gift" and not "reward"—of eternal life.

One last word on this *gifting* business, and I do so because it is a point that few are able to grasp, and this is especially true of me. Quoting now from Paul's letter to the Ephesian Church, chapter 2: 4–9:

> But God, being rich in mercy, because of the great love with which he loved us, even when we were dead in our trespasses, made us alive together with Christ—by grace you have been saved—and raised us up with him and seated us with him in the heavenly places in Christ Jesus, so that in the coming ages he might show the immeasurable riches of his grace in kindness toward us in Christ Jesus. For by grace you have been saved through faith. And this is not your own doing, it is the gift of God, not a result of works, so that no one my boast.

Eternal life means living in the presence of the Creator, a life about which we know very little. But then, it does not really matter now. We will get to that some time in the future.

Chapter Six

The Promise Maker

Within the Bible's first prophecy is also the first promise: "I will put enmity between you and the woman, and between your offspring and her offspring; **he shall bruise your head, and you shall bruise his heel**" (Genesis 3:15).

The prophecy of the enmity is clear, as is the promise, "he shall bruise your head." Bruising the head of a serpent means a death blow. At our point in history this promise is *partially* fulfilled through the victory of Christ on the cross, in which He bore our sin, becoming the sacrifice for sin, forever washing our sin into oblivion. While only partially fulfilled, it is still powerful during this interim period. But then the end will come.

In a number of places in Scripture, the final and total defeat of Satan and his legions is depicted. Here is one of these: "The devil who deceived them was thrown into the lake of fire and sulfur where the beast and the false prophet were, and they will be tormented day and night forever and ever" (Revelation 20:10).

The Promise of the Messiah to Come

Dipping back into the Books of Moses, we find the promise of a prophet like Moses. "The LORD your God will raise up for you a prophet like me from among you, from your brothers—it is to him you shall listen" (Deuteronomy 18:15).

What "a prophet like Moses" means is debated. Moses gave the Law of God. And the promised Messiah of 18:15 would likely do something similar. The Law did not bring wholeness and salvation, as we suppose it was meant to do. The Law revealed the impossibility of earning favor with God, since everyone is a law breaker. The coming prophet, meaning one who speaks the Word of God, would bring life, wholeness, and salvation.

Moses and his Torah, the first five books of the Bible, dating to around 1500 BCE,[1] are joined by prophets like Isaiah and Jeremiah who lived much later. Isaiah's date is around 750 BCE and Jeremiah's about 580. There are many other prophetic messages in the Hebrew Bible, but that is not the focus of this "little" book.

Isaiah's book is crowded with prophetic images and utterances. The most obvious are found in chapter 53. Here is a short list:

---

[1] Dates are problematic in regard to the Hebrew Bible. The 1500 BCE is a case in point. Some scholars move it forward to approximately 1350 BCE. Some think Deuteronomy was written later than Moses' period and serves as a summary of the first four books plus. One need not decide in order to see that Deuteronomy 18:15 contains a promise to come.

For he grew up before him like a young plant (v. 2).

He had no form or majesty that we should desire him (v. 2).

He was despised and rejected by men, a man of sorrows, and acquainted with grief (v. 3).

He was despised, and we esteemed him not (v. 3).

Surely he has borne our griefs and carried our sorrows (v. 4).

We esteemed him stricken, smitten by God, and afflicted (v. 4).

But he was wounded for our transgressions (v. 5).

He was crushed for our iniquities (v. 5).

Upon him was the chastisement that brought us peace (v. 5).

With his stripes we are healed (v. 5).

The Lord has laid on him the iniquity of us all (v. 6).

He was oppressed, and he was afflicted, yet he opened not his mouth (v. 7).

Like a lamb that is led to the slaughter, and

like a sheep that before its shearers is silent, so he opened not his mouth (v. 7).

By oppression and judgment, he was taken away (v. 8).

He was cut off out of the land of the living (v. 8).

Stricken for the transgression of my people (v. 8).

They made his grave with the wicked and with a rich man in his death (v. 9).

Yet it was the will of the Lord to crush him; he has put him to grief (v.10).

When his soul[2] makes an offering for sin, he shall see his offspring, he shall

prolong his days (v. 10).

And he shall bear their iniquities (v. 11).

He poured out his soul to death and was numbered with the transgressors (v. 12).

Yet he bore the sin of many, and makes intercession for the transgressors (v. 12).

Isaiah in chapter 7 speaks of a woman, a virgin, con-

---

[2] Soul means human being, human self or person, and is not some kind of spiritual particle or substance.

ceiving a son who is Immanuel, meaning "God with us" (Isaiah 7:14). Then in chapter 9 we find more:

> For to us a child is born, to us a son is given, and the government shall be upon his shoulder, and his name shall be called Wonderful Counselor, Mighty God, Everlasting Father, Prince of Peace. Of the increase of his government and of peace, there will be no end, on the throne of David and over his kingdom, to establish it and to uphold it with justice and with righteousness from this time forth and forevermore. The zeal of the LORD of hosts will do this. (vv. 6–7)

Jeremiah's chapter 31 looks forward to a new covenant, testament, or agreement that the God of Israel will establish. This rather long passage sums up the prophetic tradition:

> Behold, the days are coming, declares the LORD, when I will make a new covenant with the house of Israel and the house of Judah, not like the covenant that I made with their fathers on the day when I took them by the hand to bring them out of the land of Egypt, my covenant that they broke, though I was their husband, declares the LORD. But his is the covenant that I will make with the house of Israel after those days, declares the LORD: I will put my law within them, and I will write

it on their hearts. And I will be their God, and they shall be my people. And no longer shall each on teach his neighbor and each his brother, saying, "know the LORD." For they shall all know me, from the least of them to the greatest, declares the LORD. For I will forgive their iniquity, and I will remember their sin no more."

Jeremiah 31:31–34

There is one more prophetic piece I must add here, and that is from David, who is not usually considered a prophet, but in a number of his Psalms we cannot help but see a prophetic utterance. Note that David lived close to 1000 BCE, at a time when no nation or tribe had developed the form of execution we know as crucifixion, which apparently was developed by the Persians, later refined by the Greeks, then further perfected by the Romans. The reader must keep this in mind as key parts of Psalm 22 appear below.[3]

My God, my God, why have you forsaken me? (v. 1) This sentence was spoken by Jesus while on the cross (see Matthew 27:46).

But I am a worm and not a man, scorned by

---

[3]   King David did not experience any of that which is described in Psalm 22. The accounts of his life are laid out in Samuel and Kings.

mankind and despised by the people (v. 6).

All who see me mock me (v. 7).

He trusts in the LORD; let him deliver him; let him rescue him, for he delights in him (v. 8).

I am poured out like water, and all my bones are out of joint (v. 14).

My heart is like was; it is melted within my breast (v. 14).

My strength is dried up like a potsherd, and my tongue sticks to my haws; you lay me in the dust of death (v. 15).

For dogs encompass me; a company of evildoers encircles me (v. 16).

They have pierced my hands and feet (v. 16).

I can count all my bones—they stare and gloat over me (v. 17).

They divide my garments among them, and for my clothing they cast lots (v. 18).

How Can We Account for This?

Even a cursory examination of the material above shows that it can be accounted for in only one way: the prophets of Israel accurately pointed to a coming Messiah, and Jesus perfectly met every single prophecy.

Some will claim the prophetic material was edited after the days of Jesus to match His life story. However, no biblical scholar—Jewish, Christian, Islamic, whatever—can make this claim stick, since the manuscript evidence disputes this and makes it an impossible assertion.

It is certain that the Hebrew Bible material was published prior to Jesus' era, and we need only consider the Septuagint, the Greek translation of the Hebrew Bible, which sets in stone the books of that Bible and which dates to 180 BCE.

The thousands of extant copies of the Greek Bible, the Christian testament, reveal no evidence of reading back into the story of Jesus events that mirror the prophecies of the Hebrew Bible.

It frankly requires a very preposterous God to arrange all of what we have considered and seen in this chapter. I know it makes non-Christians uncomfortable, even anxious and fearful to even acknowledge the possibility of the truths examined here.

The Promise Maker Delivers

The unknown author of the Letter to the Hebrews starts off his masterpiece with a stunning proclamation:

> Long ago, at many times and in many ways,
> God spoke to our fathers by the prophets, but
> in these last days he has spoken to us by his

Son, whom he appointed the heir of all things, through whom also he created the world. He is the radiance of the glory of God and the exact imprint of his nature, and he upholds the universe by the word of his power. After making purification for sins, he sat down at the right hand of the Majesty on high, having become so much superior to angels as the name he has inherited is more excellent than theirs. (Hebrews 1:1–4)

The Jewish but unknown author of the piece above captured the spirit of the prophets. He lived through the time of the fulfillment of the *first-time* arrival of the Messiah. Yes, first time arrival. This Little Book speaks only of the first advent of Messiah. There will be another.

If what has been presented so far seems preposterous, it will seem even more so to find out there are three aspects, dimensions, or personages of the God of Abraham, Isaac, and Jacob.

Chapter Seven

The Creator is One in Three and Three in One

The Creator God is a Trinity, which is extraordinarily difficult to explain, and though I have attempted to do so many times, I doubt I have ever done it well.

"Three in one—or—one in three" is little more than a formula, but it expresses what is revealed about the nature of God as found in Scripture.

In the Hebrew Bible we find evidence for the triune God. In Genesis 1:1–2 we find a significant piece of the puzzle:

> In the beginning, God created the heavens and the earth. The earth was without form and void, and darkness was over the face of the deep. And the *Spirit of God* was hovering over the face of the waters.

The Hebrew word for *Spirit of God* in the passage above is *ruach* and can mean wind, breath, or spirit. Dozens of times in the Hebrew Bible *ruach* refers to Spirit, the Spirit of God.

In Isaiah 48:16 and 63:10 we find the Spirit differentiated from God yet yet the Spirit is also deity. Here is

Isaiah 63:10: "But they rebelled and grieved his Holy Spirit."

So far we have discovered two parts of the Trinity. It is not much of a stretch to acknowledge that the Creator is God. A bit of a stretch to add the "Spirit" as God also, still you have two gods then. The real trouble comes with Jesus. If He is God, then do we have three gods? How could this be expressed?

As for a third part of the Trinity, the Son, we find evidence in Psalm 2:7: "I will tell of the decree: The LORD said to me, 'You are my Son; today I have begotten you." This Psalm speaks of Christ, the Messiah, and it clearly distinguishes between the Father and the Christ.

In Psalm 110:1 we have, "The LORD says to my Lord, 'Sit at my right hand, until I make your enemies your footstool.'" The mystery found here is cleared up by seeing God as a Trinity.

Already cited is Isaiah 9:6, but because of its direct evidence for the deity of the Messiah, here is the passage again:

> For to us a child is born, to us a son is given; and the government shall be upon his shoulder, and his name shall be called Wonderful Counselor, Mighty God, Everlasting father, Prince of Peace.

Isaiah is referring to Immanuel, meaning "God with

us," from his chapter 7 verse 14, the one born of the virgin. Note the titles, "Mighty God" and "Everlasting Father," in Isaiah 9:6, which are used for God alone.

In the Greek Bible there is evidence aplenty for the deity of the Son, Jesus the Messiah, and thus, the Trinity. In Matthew 28:19–20 we find the three-part formula in the words of Jesus.

> Go therefore and make disciples of all nations, baptizing then in the name of the Father and of the Son and of the Holy Spirit, teaching them to observe all that I have commanded you. And behold, I am with you always, to the end of the age.

It has been argued that such an advanced statement of the Trinity could not have been original with Matthew but has to have been borrowed from a later period. Yet the manuscript evidence shows otherwise. There is only one textual variant in the above passage and that has to do with the use of "amen" following "age," is some old manuscripts. That is it. Codices Vaticanus, Sinaiticus, Alexandrinus, Bezae, many old Latin translations, the Vulgate, Coptic, Syriac, Armenian, Georgian, Ethiopic translations—these support the usual reading without a final *amen*.

It is this formula, originated by Jesus Himself, that firmly establishes the doctrine of the Trinity. The Creator alone is not the God of the Bible. The Son alone is not the God of the Bible. The Spirit alone is not the God of the Bible. God is Father (Creator), Son, and Holy Spirit. To leave one out is to miss the mark in defining who God is. It is as one of the ancient creeds puts it: The Three of the Trinity are co-equal, co-eternal, of one will, and of one substance.

Let Us Look a Little Further in the Greek Bible.

"In the beginning was the Word, and the Word was with God, and the Word was God" (John 1:1).

The use of the English word "was" is misleading. It is a verb of being, and is a grammatical structure known as subject nominative, and could as well be translated, "In the beginning **was and is** the Word, and the Word **was and is** with God, and the Word **was and is** God." The sentence could also be expressed as, "The Word was and is in the beginning, the God was and is with the Word, and God was and is the Word."

This Word then, *logos* in the Greek, refers to God. The Apostle John makes this clear: "And the Word became flesh and dwelt among us, and we have seen his glory, glory as of the only Son from the Father, full of grace and truth" (John 1:14). John continues in verses 17 and 18 to make it clear who the Word is:

> For the law was given through Moses; grace and truth came through Jesus Christ. No one

has ever seen God; the only God, who is at the Father's side, he has made him known.

Paul's Testimony

To prevent this chapter from becoming a tome, only two additional passages will be presented, both from the pen of Paul who in his pre-Christian life denied the deity and messiahship of Jesus vehemently. On a journey to attack Christians in Damascus of Syria, Jesus revealed Himself to Paul. No longer would Paul misunderstand. The original account of Paul's conversion is in Acts 9:1–19.

First of all, we examine what is referred to as the "kenosis" of Christ, kenosis meaning self-emptying.

> Have this mind among yourselves, which is yours in Christ Jesus, who, though he was in the form of God, did not count equality with God a thing to be grasped, but made himself nothing, taking the form of a servant, being born in the likeness of men. And being found in human form, he humbled himself by becoming obedient to the point of death, even death on a cross. (Philippians 2:5–8)

Then to the Colossian congregation, Paul has a different way of presenting Jesus' deity.

> He is the image of the invisible God, the first-

born of all creation. For by him all things were created in heaven and on earth, visible and invisible, whether thrones or dominions or rulers or authorities—all things were created through him and for him. And he is before all things, and in him all things hold together. And he is the head of the body, the church. He is the beginning, the firstborn from the dead, that in everything he might be preeminent. For in him all the fullness of God was pleased to dwell, and through him to reconcile to himself all things, whether on earth or in heaven, making peace by the blood of his cross. (Colossians 1:15–20)

Paul, trained as a rabbi by the renowned Gamaliel, knew that if Jesus was in fact the Messiah of Israel, and knowing that the religious party he belonged to, the Pharisees, had a major hand in putting Jesus to death, then his zeal was in error.

Over the course of time Paul both studied the Hebrew Bible and learned of Jesus' life and ministry, preparing him to write the passages presented above.

One last piece now, and this from John 20:24–29. The main characters are Jesus and one of the apostles, Thomas by name. The scene probably takes place in the Upper Room, that place where Jesus celebrated with His disciples what we call now the Lord's Supper.

The first time Jesus appeared, after His resurrection, to His disciples, Thomas was absent. Later, those who had seen the risen Christ told Thomas about it, but he refused to accept their story except he see Jesus alive as well. He said, "Unless I see in his hands the mark of the nails, and place my finger into the mark of the nails, and place my hand into his side, I will never believe" (John 20:25b).

Eight days later, gathered again in the same place, this time Thomas was present. Suddenly Jesus was right there and gave them the traditional greeting, "Peace be with you." Then turning to Thomas, Jesus invited him to touch the wounds on His body. Jesus said, "Do not disbelieve, but believe" (v. 27).

Thomas then said, "My Lord and my God." Jesus' response, "Have you believed because you have seen me? Blessed are those who have not seen and yet have believed" (v. 29).

For so many the most preposterous thing about Christianity has to do with the Trinity. Think of it, one yet three, three yet one. It makes no sense at all. Even when Christians believe the truth of it, we still we have a certain amount of cognitive dissonance. And this is only natural since the Trinity is ultra supernatural.

There came a time for me when I stopped fighting myself about it. Okay, I am a Christian and this is what Christians have always believed, so what is the trouble?

There is nothing in my experience that helps me accept the concept of the Trinity. It continues to be an absurd doctrine. Where I found help was in realizing that I am not the judge of God. I must, will, let God be God though I don't understand. And why should all that is God be rational to one such as I am, a limited, sinful, ignorant, and arrogant person of rather low I.Q.

I am among those Jesus referred to in John 20:29: "Blessed are those who have not seen and yet have believed."

Chapter Eight

The Predestinator

The scenario that forms the backdrop to the film "The Terminator" is beyond human capacity to visualize. Hollywood's sci-fi thriller, however, is left in the dust in the face of the "Predestinator," which is a suitable, even biblical description for the Creator God.

How is it that the God of the Bible is "The Predestinator"? Consider Romans 8:29–30:

> For those whom he foreknew he also predestined to be conformed to the image of his Son, in order that he might be the firstborn among many brothers. And those whom he predestined he also called, and those whom he called he also justified, and those whom he justified he also glorified.[1]

The Predestinator Elects

"Foreknew" simply indicates that the Creator God

---

[1] "Predestined" means predetermined or chosen. "Called" means the process of the Holy Spirit convicting of sin and revealing who Jesus is and what He did. "Justified" means to convert the sinner into a saint, making one born from above or anew. "Glorified" means the Holy Spirit has indwelt the person. God's "glory" is now *in* the believer.

knew before He even created the universe those whom He would predestine, call, justify, and glorify. Does this seem unfair?

Predestine is to predetermine.[2] Preposterous? Yes indeed. Prior to a single atom, molecule, or organism existing, the Creator already knew who would and would not come to saving faith in His Son, Jesus Christ.

I, like many Christians, despised such a notion. How awful it seemed! For twenty-nine years in active ministry I rejected the idea completely and vehemently. Then during some research I was doing in 1994, I stumbled upon the improbability, actually the impossibility, of a person being capable of saving him or herself. Scripture is clear: only the holy and righteous God forgives sin, and there is absolutely nothing anyone can do to cause or accomplish this. Only true Christianity is like this, since all the other religions of the world and a sizable portion of quasi-Christian denominations embrace nothing more than a self-help, self-save worldview, which is empty and despairing in the long run.

My initial reaction was to adopt a scenario whereby God and humans co-operate (I later learned this is referred to as "synergism"). This seemed fair. Yes, God

---

[2] Although the word "elect" or "election" is not found specifically in Romans 8:29–30 describing the sovereign work of God, it is the perfect and unifying term that sums it all up.

elected, but humans somehow accepted, or received, or agreed, which seemed to blunt the harshness of God acting alone. This satisfied me for a time, until I realized that it made a human response necessary and thus limited the decision and work of the Creator God. He is either sovereign or He is not. I could not have it both ways.

In His sovereignty, God acted unilaterally and literally in person—the Son of God, Jesus Christ, removed the believer's sin. Sin brings death,[3] and so God, the Son, died. The perfect Lamb of God, without sin, took the sinner's sin upon Himself, shed His blood, and died in the sinner's place. With sin still held on the ledger of our account, we cannot stand in the presence of God. But, predestined, called, justified, and glorified, with all our sin blotted out, we may.

A Quick Study of Election

In Genesis we find the Creator choosing Abel over Cain and Jacob over Esau, though both Cain and Esau where the first-born and should have carried the chosen line in the "normal" course of things. Abraham's second

---

[3]   How could a good and loving God allow sin to continue in His presence? Satan and the rebelling angels were cast away from the presence of God. Heaven would be no heaven were sin present. Living in our fallen world, we are stressed beyond strength trying to enjoy or even maintain life while sharing it with that which is evil.

born, Isaac, was chosen, not Ishmael the actual first-born son. Then God calls Abraham's grandson Jacob to be a people for Himself, not Esau the firstborn. This people is called Israel, and from this people would come the Messiah.

To choose is to elect is to predetermine. In the Hebrew Bible *bawkhir* is often translated as choose. Isaiah the prophet used the term in 42:1; 45:4; 64:22; and 65:9 to describe Israel. Israel is the chosen of God. Israel did not choose God.

We find election, which is the title of the doctrine of God's choosing, all through the Scripture. In the Greek Bible that we call the New Testament, we find Jesus using the word from which we get election: *eklektos* and *ekloge* in Matthew 24:22, 24, 31 and Mark 13:20, 22, 27, plus Luke 18:7, and all in reference to those whom God had chosen.

Paul uses the terms in Romans 8:33; Colossians 3:12; 1 Thessalonians 1:4; I Timothy 5:21; 2 Timothy 2:10; and Titus 1:1. Peter used the terms in 1 Peter 1:2, 6; 1 Peter 5:13; and 2 Peter 1:10. John used one of the terms in 2 John 1 and 13.

In my view, Ephesians 1:4 sums it all up: "Even as he chose (*exelexato*) us in him before the foundation of the world, that we should be holy and blameless before him." We see both "before the foundation of the world" and "in him" in the verse. We are elect *in Jesus* based on who He is and what He has done, which completely excludes anything about who we are and what we do.

God calls us to Himself—by His foreknowing, predestinating, calling, justifying, and glorifying—all under the grand and large umbrella of election.

Is this Preposterous?

The answer to the above is yes, certainly yes. How could the Creator be anything else?

For eons humans have created gods and goddesses of their own liking, but the God of Scripture is self-revealed, not created. And He is absolutely absurd.

Chapter Nine

God Dies

The title of this chapter is overly sensational, and if taken literally, is error. Obviously, God does not die; He is the ultimate Living Presence.

Still, God did die. Isaiah said it would be so as recorded in his chapter 53:

> Crushed for our iniquities
> a lamb that is led to the slaughter;
> he was cut off out of the land of the living;
> they made his grave with the wicked
> and with a rich man in his death

King David had stated the same idea two hundred and fifty years earlier: "You lay me in the dust of death" (Psalm 22:15c).

God *had* to die, since "sin when it is fully grown brings forth death" (James 1:15b). Death must come, and death is not merely dying, it is eternal separation from God in hell.[1]

---

[1] Hell may not be fire and brimstone with devils and pitch forks. Christians are divided on this point. I do not make any claim to understanding except that hell is eternal and under the domination of Satan. Whatever it is, it is not good.

At the Core of the Mystery

It was the Son of God, Jesus the Messiah, who died. God the Father did not have a child as humans do.[2] However, consider the analogy that human fathers have human sons, and the son is no less human than the father. Does this help explain Jesus, the Son of God? Not completely, but it paints a picture of a reality we can understand. Of course, we are speaking of the Trinity here, so the analogy breaks down. Nothing we know of or ever will know of while on this planet will entirely explain this mystery.

The mystery deepens: That which is not holy cannot be in the presence of the holy God—Father, Son, and Holy Spirit—yet the ultimate intention of the Godhead is that chosen, sinful humans will be with Him forever. What would be done? How could we live when the wages, the outcome of sin, is death? The answer is sin must be forgiven—washed away and cleansed by means of the death of Jesus on the cross—otherwise, I would be forever separated from the presence of God.

Abraham and Isaac

In Genesis 22 is the story of the sacrifice of Isaac. Isaac

---

[2]   Islam teaches that God had sex with the virgin Mary and that Jesus was the product of that union. This is an attempt to supplant Christian doctrine by ignoring the witness of the writers of the New Testament.

was the son of Abraham and Sarah, through whom the nation to be, Israel, would issue. Surprisingly, God, who had made it miraculously possible for Sarah to give birth to Isaac, commanded Abraham to sacrifice that very of miracle, Isaac.[3] As Abraham was about to sacrifice his son, God's angel stopped him and pointed to a ram caught in a thicket. This animal served as a substitute. Isaac lived.

God the Father gave the Son up to death, making Jesus the substitute. Only that which is holy could be a substitute.

Theologians refer to this work of God as "Substitutionary Atonement," a big term, but helpful, as it means that instead of the sinner dying, Jesus dies in that sinner's place. This is the mystery. God does what no one else can do. Since our sin is against God, only God can put away sin. And He did that on the cross. Jesus literally died in the sinner's place.

Another Look

The writer of the Book of Hebrews, in chapter 2 verse 9, provides a distinctly Jewish view of the work of Jesus on the cross.

---

[3] This event, known as the Akedah, the binding of Isaac, may be viewed as a proto-gospel, since God provides a substitute sacrifice so that the nation, the people of God, might survive.

But we see him who for a little while was made lower than the angels, namely Jesus, crowned with glory and honor because of the suffering of death, so that by the grace of God he might taste death for everyone.

We have the required number of witnesses, over a thousand-year period of time, from King David in the tenth century BCE to the first century CE, stating the very same truth. The Messiah, Jesus of Nazareth, the Son God, God in the flesh, dies.

Baptism

In the biblical perspective, baptism is a picture of what happens in the rebirthing miracle of God called conversion. To baptize is to plunge under water, to dunk, or to immerse. A person is laid back in the water, symbolizing death and burial, then is raised up again. It is not magical; no sin is washed away. Rather it is a physical re-enactment of salvation; it is storytelling.

Writing to the congregation at Colossae, Paul explains the spiritual significance of baptism:

And you, who were dead in your trespasses and the uncircumcision[4] of your flesh, God made alive together with him, having forgiven

---

[4]   Circumcision is a word used to symbolize forgiveness. Uncircumcision would refer to unforgiveness.

57

us all our trespasses, by canceling the record of debts that stood against us with its legal demands. This he set aside, nailing it to the cross. (Colossians 2:13–14)

The key phrase is "nailing it to the cross." When Jesus was crucified, God the Father placed our sin upon God the Son. Jesus emptied Himself of the glory of deity and became flesh, born of the virgin. Jesus without sin Himself became the perfect sacrifice for our sin. Jesus is the substitute, our substitute.

Paul made this truth clear to the congregation in Rome:

Do you not know that all of us who have been baptized into Christ Jesus were baptized into his death? We were buried therefore with him by baptism into death, in order that, just as Christ was raised from the dead by the glory of the Father, we too might walk in newness of life. For if we have been united with him in a death like his, we shall certainly be united with him in a resurrection like his. (Romans 6:3–5)

Baptism is not a ritual as much as it is a testimony and symbolic re-enactment of what God has done in Christ.

God died that we might not. As Paul put it, "For our sake he made him to be sin who knew no sin, so that in him we might become the righteousness of God" (2 Corinthians 5:21).

This is unimaginable love from the Triune God for the prodigals.[5]

Both preposterous and wonderful!

---

[5] A "prodigal" is one who has left his father and family to live a riotous and debauched life. See the Parable of the Prodigal Son in Luke 15:11–32.

Chapter Ten

God Lives

Jesus told His disciples on several occasions that He would die and then be raised. Matthew 16:21 recounts one such incident:

> From that time Jesus began to show his disciples that he must go to Jerusalem and suffer many things from the elders and chief priests and scribes, and be killed, and on the third day be raised.

"Killed" and "raised" both sounded impossible to Jesus' followers. Not surprisingly, Peter took Jesus aside and, Matthew tells us, "began to rebuke him saying, 'Far be it from you, Lord. This shall never happen to you'" (v. 22).

Which would have been more stunning—the killing or the raising? To Peter and the rest of the apostles, it would have been the killing, since they believed Jesus was the long-promised Messiah. As Messiah, Jesus would be king overall and invulnerable. Regarding the raising, this was secondary, since there could not be any killing.

The Gospel accounts show the disciples were completely shocked to see Jesus alive again, since His dying had so shattered their concept of who He was. They were Jews, and like most of Israel, were hoping to have the nation restored under a coming king, the Messiah. However, the nation thought of the Messiah as a military and political savior from Roman domination. Defeat of the enemy and rise of a kingdom was uppermost in their minds.

Indeed, hints of resurrection in the Hebrew Bible received little attention from the rabbis in that era.

Corruption

In Psalm 16:10, attributed to King David, is a reference that does not seem to fit David's circumstances. Many prophetic assertions in the Hebrew Bible are the same; in the midst of a text, suddenly an incongruency appears. At some point in history such strange passages, are recognized as a prophecy. Psalm 16:10 is an excellent example. "For you will not abandon my soul to Sheol, or let your holy one see corruption," is what David wrote.

"Soul" is from the Hebrew word *nephesh* and means a human being or person, not an ethereal spiritual entity. Neither would David refer to himself as "holy," and the concept of resurrection, or surviving being killed, would not be something in his awareness.

Jesus, however, did not see corruption, despite His actual death and burial. Crucified on Friday and dead at 3:00 p.m. that afternoon, He was absent from the grave early Sunday morning. Exactly when he was raised is unknown. The Apostle Peter explains:

> For Christ also suffered once for sins, the righteous for the unrighteous, that he might bring us to God, being put to death in the flesh but made alive in the spirit, in which he went and proclaimed to the spirits in prison." (1 Peter 3:18–19)

When this proclamation by Jesus took place is not cited. Historically, the resurrection is celebrated as taking place on Sunday morning, either while it was yet dark or shortly thereafter. In any case, Jesus was raised from the dead.

Jesus **was** raised; He did not raise Himself. The Father raised the Son. Paul explains it to the Corinthian congregation :

> For I delivered to you as of first importance what I also received: that Christ died for our sins in accordance with the Scriptures, that he was buried, that he was raised on the third day in accordance with the Scriptures, and that he appeared to Cephas, then to the twelve. Then he appeared to more than five hundred brothers at one time, most of who are still alive, though some have fallen asleep. Then he appeared to James, then to all the apostles. Last of all, as to one untimely born, he appeared also to me. (1 Corinthians 15:3–7)

Knowing God Is Preposterous

A Creator God who could not raise the dead would be no God at all. If the Being who is responsible for all the matter and energy that exists could not raise a dead person to life, this would be completely absurd.

Jesus *did* die, *was* raised, *did* ascend to the right hand of the Father,[1] and *will* return at the end of the age.

---

[1] To be at the right hand means to be in the position of power and authority, at minimum. It also means that the one so seated is finished with the work so designed. We speak of the "finished work of Christ."

Chapter Eleven

The Birther

The *new birth*, *born from above*, *conversion*, *salvation*, *redemption*, *reconciliation*—all are synonyms, and all are brought into being by the Birther, the Creator God.

It must be so; we simply cannot birth ourselves.

None of us birthed ourselves physically. And this is the point Jesus makes in the third chapter of John, which we examine below. We know we did not physically birth ourselves and so it is with the new birth. This is perhaps the most difficult fact that humankind has ever been faced with. Why? Because we are convinced we have to save ourselves.

The Greatest Story Ever Told

Now a look back to the early days of Jesus' ministry. A distinguished and mature leader of Israel named Nicodemus approached Jesus at night. He said to the young man, "Rabbi, we know that you are a teacher come from God, for no one can do these signs that you do unless God is with him" (John 3:2).

Jesus performed many miracles, and this did not go unnoticed by the religious leaders in Jerusalem. "What does this mean?" must have been on their minds. Could it be that this young fellow from Nazareth is someone to be reckoned with?

Whether Nicodemus came to Jesus on the sly or as an emissary from other members of the Council of Israel, the Sanhedrin, is unknown. He started with what might be referred to as flattery. Jesus stunned the learned rabbi by stating, "I say to you, unless one is born again he cannot see the kingdom of God" (John 3:3).

Nicodemus said nothing that might have inspired Jesus to say what He did. Though Nicodemus might have been looking for information, Jesus aimed straight at his heart, because He knew his heart.

Nicodemus immediately stated the impossibility of being born a second time; no going back to the mother's womb. Jesus followed up with the fact that no one can enter the kingdom of God without being born again, not even an esteemed and righteous man. Jesus cautioned Nicodemus not to be shaken by what He said and further explained that the new birth can only be accomplished by the Holy Spirit.

It is necessary to know, if we are to understand the next thing Jesus said, that the Greek word for *spirit* is the same word used for *wind* and *breath*. "The wind blows where it wishes, and you hear its sound, but you do not know where it comes from or where it goes" (v. 3:8).[1] The translation "wind" is used due to the idea of

---

[1]   The word in John 3:8 translated "wind" is the Greek word *pneuma*. It is the same word "spirit" as in Holy Spirit.

wind blowing, a sound that can often be heard, and the same can be said of the Spirit of God (see Acts 2:1–4).

What did Nicodemus hear? Jesus told him that all his wonderful righteousness could not open his eyes to see the kingdom of God. Nicodemus was actually looking at the King of the kingdom of God. No, Nicodemus would have to be birthed into that kingdom.

At the conclusion of the conversation between Jesus and Nicodemus, as related by the Apostle John, Jesus says to Him:

> As Moses lifted up the serpent in the wilderness, so must the Son of Man be lifted up, that whoever believes in him may have eternal life. For God so loved the world, that he gave his only Son, that whoever believes in him should not perish but have eternal life. (John 3:14–16)

What Nicodemus was looking for was standing right in front of him. His heart's desire, like that of all people, was to know the Creator God and live for eternity. Nicodemus was at a stage in his life when he knew that all the other enticements his decadent culture meant next to nothing.

Jesus' Words Echoed and Affirmed by the Apostle Peter

In the first letter attributed to Peter is this:

> Blessed be the God and Father of our Lord Jesus Christ. According to his great mercy, he has caused us to be born again to a living hope through the resurrection of Jesus Christ from the dead, to an inheritance that is imperishable, undefiled, and unfading, kept in heaven for you, who by God's power are being guarded through faith for a salvation ready to be revealed in the last time. (1 Peter 1:3–5)

Peter knew birthing by the Holy Spirit, who alone brings salvation, is a gift of mercy and grace, accomplished by God alone. He is the Birther.

A New Creation

Those born again, born anew, or born from above (these are synonyms) are, in Paul's lexicon, a new creation. He said, "Therefore, if anyone is in Christ, he is a new creation. The old has passed away; behold, the new has come" (2 Corinthians 5:17).

A new creation, a new race, a new people—are those birthed through the working of the Holy Spirit who reveals to us our sinful nature and the Savior, all for the purpose of preparing us to be re-birthed.

Always and Forever Unimaginable

Saved by grace reigns as the very most preposterous concept. And why? We simply cannot come to grips with the fact that we cannot earn the favor of God is some manner. In our attempts to do so we must lapse into some form of agnosticism or atheism. I have often said that if I were not a Christian I would certainly be an atheist.

All the religions of the world save Christianity provide paths, ways, means, or directions that a human can pursue to obtain some ultimate goal. Herein are the counterfeit means of salvation, which lead to nothing more than deception and hopelessness. To be saved, redeemed, converted, born again—is something only the Holy Spirit of God can do.

Chapter Twelve

In the Presence of the Triune God

Who would not be shocked to hear that the ultimate intention of the Creator God is to be forever present with those He made in His image? "Far beyond the wildest imagination" does not express the utter preposterousness of such a concept.

We humans have difficulty being in the presence of one another for extended periods of time, however strong the bond. There are exceptions, surely, but overall, I suspect that for the majority of us loving togetherness for ever and ever is questionable.

Many Rooms

During the closing days of Jesus' earthly ministry, He had long talks with His disciples. Part of one conversation that suits our purpose is John 14:1–3:

> Let not your hearts be troubled. Believe in God, believe also in me. In my Father's house are many rooms. If it were not so, would I have told you that I go to prepare a place for you? And if I go and prepare a place for you, I will come again and will take you to myself,

that where I am you may be also.

After three-plus years of following Jesus, seeing Him raise the dead, heal all manner of illnesses, cast out demons, and break the fundamental laws of nature by multiplying food in vast quantities, walking on water, and calming storms with his command, they knew His word was not to be doubted. No, He would not lie to them or give them false comfort.

The Marriage Supper of the Lamb

The Church, that invisible Body of believers known only to God, is referred to as the Bride of Christ. The word "church" in the Greek is *ekklesia* and is feminine in form.

Jesus is the bridegroom. He referred to Himself as such in Matthew 9:15: "And Jesus said to them, 'Can the wedding guests mourn as long as the bridegroom is with them? The day will come when the bridegroom is taken away from them, and then they will fast.'"

One of the last parables Jesus gave to His disciples is the parable of the wedding feast. It is found in Matthew 22:1–14, and in it He painted the picture of a wedding feast. The second coming of Jesus at the end of the age is likened to a bridegroom coming to take His bride away. And when this happens there will be a wedding feast, or as it is spoken of in the book of Revelation, a marriage supper:

Then I heard what seemed to be the voice of a great multitude, like the roar of many waters and like the sound of mighty peals of thunder crying out,

> "Hallelujah!
> For the Lord our God
> the Almighty reigns.
> Let us rejoice and exult
> and give him the glory,
> for the marriage of the Lamb has come;
> and his Bride has made herself ready;
> it was granted her to clothe herself
> with fine linen, bright and pure"—
> for the fine linen is the righteous deeds of the saints.
> (Revelation 19:6–8)

The Bride then joins the Bridegroom, and they are happily united forever. Here now is what was revealed to the Apostle John as found in Revelation 21:1–4:

> Then I saw a new heaven and a new earth, for the first heaven and the first earth had passed away, and the sea was no more. And I saw the holy city, new Jerusalem, coming down out of heaven from God, prepared as a bride adorned for her husband. And I heard a loud voice from the throne saying, "Behold, the dwelling place of God is with man. He will dwell with them, and they will be his people,

and God himself will be with them as their God. He will wipe away every tear from their eyes, and death shall be no more, neither shall there be mourning nor crying nor pain anymore, for the former things have passed away."

The promise of the ultimate triumph of the "offspring" of the woman, depicted in Genesis 3:15, is fulfilled. By means of the completed work of Jesus the Messiah, the Word become flesh, God become flesh, that atoning death for sin, then the resurrection, and finally the ascension to heaven, the dwelling place of God, there is a Bride, the Church.

No longer east of Eden, no longer in a world torn and tortured, no longer in the presence of that hideous strength, Satan and his demons—no, it is paradise restored.

It seems fitting to close with words that Paul wrote to the Church at Corinth:

Yet among the mature we do impart wisdom, although it is not a wisdom of this age or of the rulers of this age, who are deemed to pass away. But we impart a secret and hidden wisdom of God, which God decreed before the ages for our glory. None of the rulers of this age understood this, for if they had they would not have crucified the Lord of glory.

But, as it is written, "What no eye has seen, nor ear heard, nor the heart of man imagined, what God has prepared for those who love him"—these things God has revealed to us through the Spirit, for the Spirit searches everything even the depths of God.

And so it will be forever and ever, says the Preposterous God. Amen!

The Preposterous God: a Summary

The mostly unknown God is preposterous and unimaginable, and thus it is beyond our human capacity to define Him. Yet we read in Ecclesiastes 3:11b, "He has put eternity into man's heart, yet so that he cannot find out what God has done from the beginning to the end."

Solomon, the likely author of Ecclesiastes in the Hebrew Bible, gives us the above verse in the tenth century before the Common Era. We ask, "What did he mean?"

We have a sense of what might be referred to as a Godness buried deep within us. Genesis 1:27 contains a staggering revelation: "So God created man in his own image, in the image of God he created him, male and female he created them."

The Creator God constructed us humans, male and female, and in His image. Thus, one can legitimately say the Creator God of the Bible is both male and female and who implanted the quest to know Him[1] within us, perhaps in our DNA. Quite amazing yet unimaginable!

---

[1]   I use Him rather than Him/Her in this Final Note.

Despite an inner awareness of something greater than ourselves, a God concept, this does not give us a revelation of who God is or what God is like. Our understanding is, to say the least, extremely limited. Smart as we are, aware as we are—these only take us so far. Thus, the absolute necessity for revelation.

God in Person

Some two thousand years ago, a tried and tested elderly apostle of Jesus wrote, "In the beginning was the Word,[2] and the Word was with God, and the Word was God" (John 1:1). Was it the author's intent to remind the reader of Genesis 1:1, "In the beginning God created the heavens and the earth"?

The Word, *logos* in Greek, is God. God is the Word, a word spoken to us and buried deep within us. For long millennia, the sound of the word was muffled, faint, confused, and illegible.

Yet we humans searched, and searched hard, to hear the Word. How close we came to an accurate decipher is an unanswerable question. No matter how hard we tried, we could not get there. Therefore, the Word Himself showed up.

---

[2]   The word "was" in Greek is a subject nominative and does not have a sense of time. It can be rendered, "was and is" or simply "is."

"And the Word became flesh and dwelt among us, and we have seen his glory, glory as of the only Son from the Father, full of grace and truth" (John 1:14).

The apostle Paul put it this way: "When the fullness of time had come, God sent forth his Son" (Galatians 4:4).

This Word gave us this word: "I am the way, and the truth, and the life. No one comes to the Father except through me" (John 14:6).

All the foregoing is preposterous, but what would one expect from a preposterous God?

Who Is the Word? What Did the Word Do?

"Name" in ancient or Biblical Hebrew has double components. The name is derived from both who a person is and what the person did.

For instance, Daniel means "one given by God," and Daniel was a prophet to the nation of Israel while they were captive to the Babylonians in the sixth century before the Common Era. The name Daniel refers to who Daniel was and what he did.

Joshua is another example. The name means "Yahweh saves," and Joshua, Moses' second-in-command, led the Israelites, the chosen people of God, across the Jordan and into the Promised Land.

Jesus, the name, is derived from Joshua via several

languages, first Hebrew, then Greek, then Latin, finally English. Jesus or Joshua—the names mean that Yahweh or God saves or brings salvation. It was long thought that the Messiah, or Christ, meaning the one appointed by God, would be named Jesus. In the first century of the Common Era, many Jewish mothers named their sons Jesus.

In the sixth century BCE, the Hebrew prophet Isaiah received a word from God about a coming Messiah: "Therefore the Lord himself will give you a sign. Behold, the virgin shall conceive and bear a son, and shall call his name Immanuel" (Isaiah 7:14). Immanuel means "God come to be with us" in person. Two chapters later we find, "For to us a child is born, to us a son is given, and the government shall be upon his shoulder, and His name shall be called Wonderful Counselor, Mighty God, Everlasting Father, Prince of Peace."

This is surely a preposterous God. Yet, a God who speaks the entire universe into existence should be able to pull off such a task.

Jesus, the son of the Virgin Mary, is this God with us. Paul put it this way: "But when the fullness of time had come, God sent forth his son, born of woman, born under the law, to redeem those who were under the law, so that we might receive adoption as sons" (Galatians 4:4–5). The writer of Hebrews wrote, "Long ago, at many times and in many ways, God spoke to our fathers by the prophets, but in these last days he has spoken to us by his Son, whom he appointed the heir of all things" (Hebrews 1:1–2).

We see who Jesus is. Now, what did He do? "To redeem" goes directly to the doing. Jesus' death on the cross, prophesied centuries earlier (See Psalm 22 and Isaiah 53), was the substitute for the death that sin finally brings to all. There Jesus took our sin away in a manner we will never completely understand.

The title *Savior* means that Jesus takes our sin away and gives us the gift of eternal life. His resurrection seals the work of the Savior. This Savior, this Redeemer, will return at a time no one knows to restore us to fellowship with the Creator God, which is the ultimate intention of the Triune God, Father, Son, and Holy Spirit.

Preposterous but true!

www.ingramcontent.com/pod-product-compliance
Lightning Source LLC
Chambersburg PA
CBHW071839020426
42331CB00007B/1790